THE OLD DOMINION

The Old Dominion

Poems by

Jennifer Key

University of Tampa Press

Epigraph lines from "Canary" are taken from
Grace Notes, W. W. Norton & Co., Inc., © 1989 by Rita Dove.
Reprinted by permission of the author.

Manufactured in the United States of America
Printed on acid-free paper -
First Edition

The University of Tampa Press
401 West Kennedy Boulevard
Tampa, FL 33606

ISBN 978-159732-107-5 (hbk.)
ISBN 978-159732-108-2 (pbk.)

Browse & order online at
http://utpress.ut.edu

Library of Congress Cataloging-in-Publication Data
Key, Jennifer, 1974-
[Poems. Selections]
The old dominion : poems / by Jennifer Key. -- First edition.
    pages cm
Includes bibliographical references.
ISBN 978-1-59732-107-5 (hbk : acid-free paper) --
ISBN 978-1-59732-108-2 (pbk : acid-free paper)
I. Title.
PS3611.E967O43 2013
811'.6--dc23   2013007095

Contents

For G.C.

I

Fact is, the invention of women under siege
has been to sharpen love in the service of myth.

If you can't be free, be a mystery.

—Rita Dove, "Canary"

Still Life with Jackie O

The beautiful shed skins of Mrs. Kennedy are on display at the Corcoran
    Gallery of Art,
and all of Washington wanders through her closets.
The French call still-lifes *une nature morte*, the gender always female.

This is the bright showroom of her life where her careful glamour is undone
under track-lighting muted as the moonlight wash of satin on a woman's hip.
Perfection pleases us. We pick it over happiness.

The art of being a woman has always been discretion.
Kid gloves over bitten nails, dark glasses, the triple-strand
pearls. Each obscures a certain worry.

Seduction is suggestion rather than sex itself, a mirror
in which the body seems to shimmer. Her absence whispers
a caesura of sound, that breathless quality we loved. She holds

her breath. The mannequins wait, prim as petticoats,
on their translucent legs and appropriate pumps.
Their hair, sheer tulle, combed and bobbed.

Only the perfect grammar of her gowns remains,
their clipped Potomac lockjaw and horsy girls' school hemlines,
seams square as Chippendale railing.

Even her dressing room's been boxed neat as a sonnet.
The glittering foil of jewelry and Lilly Daché hats
all pretty and all under glass.

What Jackie loved best were the Greeks—their endless incarnations.
When the gods descended as a swan or rain,
whatever form they needed to take, they could.

[5]

Between Us the Sea: Circe's Aubade

"But Odysseus remained true in his heart."
            −Homer

He who burns for Ithaca and not for me
    now sails for home and a wife whose deception
        is demurely domestic. What matter if

another nymph with glossy braids
    should sway him from his way?
        Nights when the Aegean is a silver platter of light,

what can I do but fold and unfold my trousseau
    of longing under our bridal canopy,
        old sea nets swathed against the gnats?

Memory, loyal dog, pants at my heels.
    He has his hound, I mine.
        The waves turn their wine dark pages

and the days advance.
    What I have become or will
        remains unwritten on the palimpsest of my life.

Who knows better than a woman how to turn
    into whatever poor beast the stunned heart wills?
        He was for a time my strong stag striding,

his antlers, wet velvet, moss.
    Now others, mere pets, persist in their pens,
        hide and haunch heavy with tick and flea,

pining for themselves and the men they used to be,
  their minds alone keen as they were before.
    They bray and bleat all night at unnamed stars,

which are neither great nor gallant, only abundant.
  Wheeling overhead: no Orion, no hunter, no belt to unbuckle.
    They are nothing to a goddess like me—

a shawl of stars the earth wears
  and the constellation we might have been
    inscribed each moment on the waves before it breaks apart.

Circe and Her Lovers in a Landscape

—Dosso Dossi, oil on canvas, c. 1525

It was a trick of sweetness, honey,
mulled wine that made them mine.
Their wives, the chieftains' daughters,
always wanted more. Only I wanted less.

Look at it this way: I'm honest if nothing else.
When I called them *Dear* or *Pet*,
I meant it literally.
To come and go, men call it freedom—

I, a sentence. Who wants
to be homesick, longing for a lifetime?
The lesson learned too late of love's design:
it harnesses us or us it—a bit we bite,

or else alone grind down our teeth at night.
Do not imagine that they miss their brides,
those bartered beauties, bright gardens
they plowed every now and then.

On the white horn of my beach,
I tend to each swaggering
sailor who yearned to leave his past behind.
I curry their newfound fur swirled

like a current whipped to whirlpool,
let them lick milk from my open hand.
I recover the selves they lost
not just in mind but in the body too.

The few who were soft and doting in their lives,
here they step, spotted fawns in a filigree of fern,
but if they were coarse and greedy, boarish brutes,
I let them root for fodder in their sties.

The ones who were cocksure,
lifting their legs on every rock in sight?
The mutts who roved wherever noses led?
See how the collar of companionship domesticates

mild spaniels curled on cushions, how
the muzzled whips of greyhounds neither bark nor bite—
Ah, how like a human to pity a dog on a leash
when not one of you is free

in your own mortal cage of carnivorous bones.
Cave canem: beware the rabid cur in your own heart.
You think that you're its master, but you're not.
I teach my animals constancy, control,

the shroud we women weave,
content with whatever the proverbial
dog drags in. Think of Penelope,
persistent as the great taproot of her bed,

then think of Helen
once the whitewater of desire spit her back
to that same shore from which she strayed.
The song she sings these days: *Forgive, Forgive—*

Do I look like the type to apologize for anything?
I, flesh alone in a forest of fur,
only wanted them to feel themselves as muscle
while all the world saw them as meat

on which a blade might fall at any time.
I wanted loyalty, for my loves to stay
obedient, enchanted to enchanter,
as faithful as the water to the shore.

You see, I made them animal
to make them half human.
If I wanted them wild,
I would have left them man.

The Apprenticeship of Jelly Roll Morton

— Romare Bearden,
collage of various papers with ink,
graphite, and surface abrasion on fiberboard
sight: 24.1 x 34.9 cm (9 ½ x 13 ¾)

No Eden, Storyville.
No green thought in a green glade here,
where sometimes night is a black palm
sweating at the window and other times
just a knuckled claw reaching through

this shotgun shack in the Quarter.
Bearden got it right.
The women are only background,
where they bend to retrieve their drawers
and striped stockings where they fell,

and the bottle of hothouse hooch,
Raleigh Rye, sways on the upright.
Out on Gravier Street, catcalls
shatter like glass, and the late moon,
old yellow tom, hooks his claw,

but here Jelly Roll swoops and stomps
a jazz so good it answers its own questions
and makes the live oaks let down their hair
of heat lightning and Spanish moss.
Each note's an amen to the one that came before—

he plays like a preacher working a tent revival
when your soul is simply burning like venom
to be saved. Brother, sister, come to me, Lord,

Lord. The women pull off or on their dresses
depending who's coming or going while

that Wurlitzer wails and its keys go on talking
to each other. The way he plays, the way
he plays, those women could almost save themselves.
No Jesus, no deliverance but his—
not today, they know, when the small of their backs

is a knot of fever and ache and those orchids
tucked in their hair do nothing
but wilt behind one ear.
Still, as long as those hands are walking,
their future's a reverie

run up the keyboard on one hand.
The way Jelly Roll plays,
it won't be long until those women—
like Lazarus, conjure women each—
rise and walk the waters off the Gulf.

Honeymoon in the New World

– For G.C.

We sailed at dawn, newborn colonists
with our rings locked in the safe
and the bright blade of the Caribbean
honing itself on the beach.

For us the world waits
wasp-waisted as a bride,
ours alone in her tourniquet of tulle
with so many layers left to lift.

We've come to find paradise
but find others like ourselves instead,
advancing empires of two along the equator.
Our side of the Huguenot wall:

A kingdom of conch and plantain,
the breadfruit's doughy heart
we cook and call our own.
The island wears her black bracelet of sea

carelessly, a clanging cuff of salt and surf.
Here, sun-scored couples toast
that ancient marriage of convenience—
beauty and brutality.

How else to admire the canebrake's banner
but not the men and mules haunch-high in hunger?
In this month even the moon burns
shadows through the palm leaves,

silvers water in the wells offshore,
and stutters through the shutter across the floor
(a wildfire, and our hearts, timber
about to catch).

My darling, now that we've reached the green shore,
where loss waits like a promise we have made,
what are we to do with this country we carve
late beneath our veil of mosquito netting

when one of us is certain to rule alone at the end?
Even now night steps from her silken gown
of heat and light and approaches without shame,
like a girl who thinks it is enough to be beautiful—

Lesson

In the version we were told, she deserved it.
A girl dumb enough to be tricked

by her grandmother's calico sleeping cap.
Didn't his fangs glisten in the dark,

constant as the crust of salt along the shore?
No matter. Her death had to happen

so that children could cheer the uncanny huntsman
who knew well enough to slice her from wolf gut

as though all good girls were meant to rise again
and again and women were merely the resurrected flesh

of what was once blind faith and obedience.
Only older, did we know that she chose

to enter that leafy evening of fir tree and oak,
the linden and sycamore with their alabaster arms.

Behind her, fields of flax folded themselves
in sunshine and wind, and farther back still

her mother stood and wept,
but where the girl stepped was knotted

in thicket and thorn. Trees shivered
their green music high overhead.

She knew it was not tragedy to live a while
in that lush pocket of shadow, even if she became

the first of many who walked towards the one they loved
and found the wolf instead. How else to explain? Desire

was unlearning every fear she'd been taught.
Take, eat, she said to the world. And he did.

Red Nails

High school girls are good
at bringing a brilliant hunger to their bodies.
Their idea of womanhood, a *trompe l'oeil*:
legs whittled to a wishbone of happiness and desire,
hair spun blonde as a sugar cookie.

In the splinter of Upper South,
expensive, fertilized fields glitter with frost.
The girls bloom big-headed as the dying lilies,
a lush lacework on the surface of Black Pond.
October's scalp glows auburn, incandescent.

Everything burning and beautiful must shed itself and vanish.
From here, the Blue Ridge is only a ledge of color—
a lip, as in a Rothko painting, deep blue that bleeds
into smoke-white air, the color of exhaust and cement
sound barriers between the Beltway and the woods.

Here, girls grow lean as late light
while they perfect longing and call waiting
in the starter castles of Northern Virginia—
their bodies not made to hide secrets
but to disclose them, each and every one.

The Girl in Your Picture

with her unzipped jeans straddled low
on her hips, or the one in tight tee
and camo pants, cutie pie with a .22,
face slicked to the barrel
she can't get close enough to,
or the girl in the room next door,
in a haze of Effexor as comfortable
as a cotton muumuu she'll slip out of
maybe for you, murmuring shoot this one
belly button down, the one who's back flat,
sleeping days through the phone
and silverware slammed away,
or even more T and A, say stood up,
this time against a tree, in a bikini,
leggy, rouged, with pony tails;
or getting it on with all her happiness in this one;
or topless, all tits and torso, no head;
or bent over, bowling with both hands;
or cocooned in bed linen, sheet for a dress,
eyes slit as blinds;
or shopping for an apartment building
with no shrubbery around doors and windows;
or my friend afraid of the dark and
rechecking locks and still unable to sleep;
or the one folding and unfolding her drug enclosure leaflet,
the doll with side effects, the drunk in heels,
the chick in bed with a guy saying
Let's keep this between us;
or that happy ending when he leaves at six a.m.
and she doesn't move for two days;
or the way you look at the girl in the room
next to me when she can't get out of bed

is not about seduction.
It's about you and what you want when you say
lie down on your back,
let me take
your picture.

Minnesota Multiple Personality Indicator, et al.

Just to be sure you lie compulsively,
answer: True False, I never lie.
For the sake of the alcoholic, the drug user,
hidden children in us all,
fill in the corresponding oval: True False,
I have some habits that are damaging.

So that there won't be any doubt as to
what we're up against, please answer
what it means to hear your father in the night
kitchen scrape open the bread crisper
and sandy the floor with crumbs.

A) Did he guide his walk with hall light,
living room lamp, and there in the kitchen leave
the icebox door gaping wide? or,
B) Did he close the gap between bed and
bread by instinct alone? If you chose B.,
is it because some things you just know,
like hunger, sleeplessness, and where
to find crackers?

Be still and let us throw a noose
around you, and while you wait,
shade-in the bubble grid to show
the landscape in your head
no wider than a moth's wingspan
or a small leaf littering the bottom stair,
on which it seems there's nothing there at all.

For, dear girl, you have done this before,
channeled past ottoman and chair,
straight through the kitchen and outside
into the cricket-humming wash,
where you do not entirely dissolve
like a sugar into water, but—it's true—
a new distance opens up, laps you.

Desire 1

Baltimore April and a chill rain for days.
In a yard up North Charles, slick leaves blanket flower beds,
daffodils rustle, licking their yellow tongues.
The sky tightens to metal: it will be cold for days

while the world sleeps, fat in her green bed.
A geranium on the nightstand purses her lipsticked mouth.
Her domesticated wilderness quiets my heart that,
like a house cat, learns to be content in a contained place.

I'll walk to the museum and look at Matisse,
his beautiful, drowsy rooms. In one, a vase of anemones
breathes. In another, a woman who expects nothing—
no one comes to run his fingers up her thighs.

Not yet noon, the day softens like an apple,
a brown sweater knits through the branches.
It's the body Matisse loved to paint—
his famous nude finished

so that at last there might be
this hothouse sheen of a woman alone
on canvas. Her body remained
once all else was gone.

Desire 2

Want wears me out.
Coffee and bed barely get made by noon.
In the yard, winter bulbs begin
to rise from their still beds.

The sun slides on the frost-white ground,
through the window and across my cat, stretching—
a fastening, unfastening gold bracelet
on the hardwood floor.

If it were only feeling one's way,
then who would want it?
Spring is a slow season:
a wilderness about to happen.

When I do get up, two eggs in the frying pan,
cool, liquid continents,
slowly warm and harden
into something good to eat.

Anniversary

– For G.C.

Because when we embarked we stood beside
a cake tall as your average three-year-old
and I was too busy with the blade in my hand
and a blueprint of dismantling in my head,

determined to dissect iced trellises
of sugar and clip rosebuds spun from butter
to let your hand find its home along the hollows
a hip makes, at this embarkation I will be

less obsessed with the geometry of beauty
(my whole life I've tried to solve for *y*),
more meanderer than arrow, more meadow
than hedgerow, growing the way the tulips

you planted our first fall broke open, black
saucers full of evening for us to lap
in our unfolding origami of bedclothes—
that privacy that bloomed because of you.

II

In the beginning, all America was Virginia.

– William Byrd II

Jefferson's Daughters

Snow is falling
on the age of reason, on Tom Jefferson's
little hill and on the age of sensibility.

— Robert Haas, "Monticello"

And it's drafty in his house of enlightenment
with its many windows on the wilderness
    and its domed oculus an unblinkered eye on high,
where his daughters who have been to Paris

    cannot travel to Richmond for a dance—
their phaeton's skeleton too delicate
    for the rutted roads blue with snow and shade—
they, who have walked the halls of Palladio

    and watched North America—Virginia, really,
its shores salted with tobacco and slavery,
    scrub pine and saltback, recede
behind a scalloped wall of waves

    like an immigrant's dream in reverse,
borne back into the dark folds of France's catholic habits,
    where Maria, the image of her long-dead mother
and namesake of the Virgin Mother herself,

    wanted to convert—well, here they are
nearly cloistered at nineteen, snowbound
    in their father's great georgic experiment
while the social season whirls without them,

and the sisters grow spiny as fiddlehead ferns,
their foreheads pressed to the plate-glass walls,
    truer terrarium than house these days.
So early they look to the windows to find

    the thin ghosts of themselves staring back.
Their quick steps on the stairs,
    a ladder jackknifed and narrow,
are minced as minuets they turn in time

    to the tinny cymbal of the gong
which rings in house and field alike.
    Do not pity them this,
slighted by American abstraction,

    freedom for a few and all that.
Know that if there are locks in the house
    (and there are)
they at least hold the key

    as mistress over all but mostly larder and cellar,
where the tongues of bells clang incessantly,
    their days wound tight as the Great Clock itself.
Oh, if there is a god here,

    he enters the kitchen weekly
to wind the hands and let it go.
    Maria and Martha travel whole days
on the tethered length of needle and thread.

They embroider miles in the stitching
and backstitching of a cushion,
    and perhaps they are content
in their kingdom of two.

    Someone, after all, has to dust the jawbone of history
in the entrance hall—that curiosity cabinet
    of the continent, contained and arrayed:
map, mineral, & mastodon,

    proof of a past they can only imagine
and evidence of the land where they live
    but barely see—
their horizon clipped by cloud and privilege.

    Poised as they are on the cusp of the country,
practically curtsying on the precipice of wilderness,
    they stay indoors instead to watch
the antlers in the front hall branch and grow

    on walls by candlelight
and the clock's cannonball plummet
    into the dark understory until
first light drags another weight,

    groaning, into dawn when they must rise,
as their absent father bid them be
    alert to survey his *workhorse of nature*,
the terraced gardens iced as wedding cake.

There is always work waiting to be done.
Men and women, dutiful as dumbwaiters,
    ferry water and wood.
Outside the monument snow falls on

    the shallow pond with its fish locked in ice
and the fox curled in his dark den of desire,
    dreaming of spring, for the age of reason
to finally see the light.

    In the ornamental forest of the grove,
the seed pods of magnolias are packed tight.
    The old dominion drowses half-asleep,
the fist of her buds less blossom than bomb.

The Norfolk and Western

– For S.T.

I am standing in the abandoned passenger station
that has stood for years like a stain
on the dragging skirt of Hotel Roanoke.
It is still 1953, before the last steam engine rolled

out of town, taking with it the world as it was.
On the wall the timetable marks the pending arrival
of the Birmingham Special and the Tennessean,
of the Powhatan Arrow with its monogrammed china clinking

and sleeping cars rocking, each rounding the mountain
for the empty rail yard below—its creosote ties shine
black as the coal veins in the hills.
Let this building be the elegy

for lost trains that ran through lost towns
when coal was king, company towns
with their abandoned Chevrolet dealerships
and feed stores, their P.O.'s and trestles

suspended like ghost limbs along the route.
Each a town called Solitude,
or Rural Retreat, Green Cove, Cripple Creek—
hollows along the line illuminated in the single exposure

of the train's yellow eye, bright as a bullet.
Those towns floated for an instant
on a crinoline of steam before the trains charged past.
Somewhere out in the night even now you may hear

the No. 78 screaming out of Abingdon for Petersburg,
flying forever beneath its white plume of nimbus cloud.
The cattle driven to pasture pause, and the old plow horse bows
her head when it quickens the air and muscles through her field.

A couple, standing on the porch, listens to the engine roar
before quiet falls like a curtain at the end of an act
and the summer grass begins to sing again.
At last its whistle wails high lonesome at the edge

of the Iaeger Drive-In, where lovebirds pretend to watch
tonight's feature, in which—at this very moment—
a plane flies into the dead corner of the screen and seems,
miraculously, to disappear before the train does.

Delay at Washington National

April 2007

The flags these days are always at half-mast.
Enlisted men and women grown fatigued
in uniforms the shade of sand and mortar, wars
no one can win, supposedly are mustering

or, rather, sit and stare inside the terminal
of Reagan National. Our flight is stalled as well
by silver screens of rain that cordon off
our coast. Wet weather in the heartland holds

us here. No shadow falls except the Monument's,
a sundial ticking down the hours until dark.
Who knows how long our narrow rows must wait?
The child a row ahead repeats her endless *whys,*

and sunlight, firing in flashes, ricochets
across the river's tongue that forks this spit
of jetty and the Capitol—America's
own Pantheon, its marble layers stacked

like cake for congressmen to slice and serve.
The fathers of our country can't be found;
instead, the boys in cufflinks play at war,
their sandbox half the way across the world.

Lords of pork, lapel pins, legislation;
Pater Familias to beltway wives
swanning in suits the color of lipstick;
well-heeled progenitors of rustbelt states

and sons in seersucker who do not kneel
but prep under St. Alban's cross upon the Mount,
this season swathed in sweet wisteria
that weeps alone for those unblessed by birth, the rest

who shall not harden here on velvet playing fields
but once deployed grow wiser in the awful grace
of God (who, it's said, must be on our side).
At last the engines rumble, gunned to life:

the flight attendant's cue to take the stage
and pantomime procedures for takeoff.
Any moment now we'll rise above entrenched moats
of Metro churning underground or Zoo,

where moms with strollers watch orangutans.
The stewardess, Tippi Hedren honey-blond
and alabaster-cool, rehearses her escape.
She pirouettes in navy pumps; we see

her updo's swirl, a cyclone pinned in place.
How casual survival when in flight!
Even her navy ascot's earned its wings.
She flashes us her smile, which disappears

beneath a yellow mask. *To start the flow
of oxygen inhale.* But I'm already slouched
against the window's plastic curve to watch
spring-green Virginia crenellate before

I number every sailboat on the Bay
that writes the wind onto the waves in wakes,
a trail of Vs chalked white and soon erased.
The stewardess strolls our rows to demonstrate

the proper way to clutch a cushion just in case.
In case of water landing (in which case we won't
be landing) *for your safety we're equipped*—
The child begins to bang her sippy cup.

Attention, please, for just a minute, folks!
She wants to show us how to save ourselves,
but we've been belted in for so damned long
the lot of us just stares, too tired to look up.

Autumns

I return to the drowned creek
of memory where two currents wash,
saline and fresh, the past and this year's.

When the hillside sparks a tinder
of electric filaments sheer to the Potomac,
I walk the deer paths in the roan-colored woods.

Gone now the undertow of creeper and sumac;
gone, too, the lost loves I thought would break
my heart in two. A hundred fires flame up golden

among the branches and wait
to be extinguished. Rain will come—
the small pinecones unlock their careful cages

and unfold. Soon, the thumbprint of ice
will quiet Black Pond, and I think
I might always be content

to name the beautiful things of this world
with the word *loss*.
Who else would be so foolish

as to welcome her own undoing every year?
Listen, the flickering leaves cackle and call
as they toss down their heavy burdens,

Will you never be happy?
All summer you have been loved
and it still was not enough.

West Virginia

In a bathtub in Hiko, West Virginia,
my figure inverts in the faucet's gleam,
fabricating the lie that the body is a thing
just as likely to show up here as anywhere.
Consciousness tempers a bit with water,
like my plastic cup of bourbon and ginger
translucent now with melted ice.
A trance of silence from the hotel hall
whirs in the ventilation fan.
I'd like to leave this reflection behind
in the unmade bed as though this happened
a long time ago and I had to look hard
to find the person I was then again.
Instead, I water myself down
with some new trick or other
and see the horizon as the brick heel of a house
where a lawnmower hums out back.
What can any of us know about ourselves
except that we're good for filling out
the sleeves of our shirts?
Still, today at a pumpkin fair in southern Ohio,
I saw a man lift a meanly glowing beauty
by his teeth.

Evening on the River

My father says he'll take me down the James.
He doesn't want to ask what's wrong with me.
Instead, he'll show me how to rise above
the riverbed and water pulling down.

The current skims along, reptilian black.
I think of you. My mind's a riverbank
that holds within something that can't be seen.
It's no great loss what I've become this year.

I'll skim above the trees; their bodies wash
below us in the tide. For what is there
to lose? Their black-green leaves and trunks rush back:
the water knits their broken bodies whole.

Imagine all the trees that soon will sink
as sunlight tightens up its girth across the sky.
I think of you and how there's more to this
than water, trees, or why I float apart.

I think of you. Always these thoughts become
a cold, black field of water underfoot.
We're carried down the river to the end,
where afternoon soon winnows into night.

Its darkness is a pane of glass for me,
for water's just another thing that has
a lining with a constant racing flood,
an undercurrent surfacing at last.

Molotov Cocktail

I never wanted to play the drinking game "I Never,"
in which a girl I knew once upped the odds,
said *I never tried to kill myself* then sat back
and watched whomever drank confess to suicide

not carried to term. I didn't want any part
of this cryptic heartache over rum and coke,
information served, tossed back neat as a shot.
A statement like this assumes everybody wants

to drain her conscience like grease from bacon,
fat from soup, sadness I let curdle
from the whole milk of me. A statement like this
is not a pack of dirty playing cards

your roommate brings you from Greece,
no tidbit for Trivial Pursuit:
What famous catcher was on the winning team
of the 1976 World Series? What close friend

spent summer evenings on railroad tracks,
trying to carry it off?
It's not a game like Twister,
put your confession on this red dot,

bend yourself backwards towards the blue,
a fun, get-to-know-ya kinda game.
It's not a pastime like bingo at the VFW Hall,
five minutes in the closet, truth or dare.

Do you want to know about wanting to die?
It's a light left burning somewhere in the house,
a light you rise to find and turn off again.
At six a.m., daylight bruises purple

and all day long folds, unfolds you
like an accordion of paper dolls. Wear this out.
Go back to start. Turn around in mid-stream.
There are children starving in Ethiopia.

There are panhandlers at the end of your block.
There are people who'd gladly take your life;
your problem is you happen to be one of them.
Carry on like everyone around you, start

what your doctor calls Processing:
Wear a smile. Have a nice day,
the happy ending we all knew you had in you,
the Graduation day. At a bridal shower,

the bride is lifting a Teflon muffin pan
from a white pastry of tissue paper.
In the kitchen, bridesmaids sliver crust from bread,
layer slices of cucumber.

Today's theme is integration of the old and new,
something borrowed, something blue.
A fire is lit beneath the fondue;
it simmers on slow boil. Make yourself

busy: start collecting trash and then arrange
what's left of the mess for the guests to look at.
Inside you're antiseptic as an airport.
You could be anywhere.

Resolution in Winter

I've given up sleep's slow work before.
Once last winter I threw in the towel
and went running in the middle of the night.
Part of me remained pinched in sleep,
soft as meat in a lobster's claw.
The other part did what I had to do
and went into the floodplain of stars.
My lifeline forked a ridge of scrub pine
and a gutted cornfield
while my breathing churned monotonous
in its black chest of water.
I heard an animal, sudden silver,
move beyond the pine.

Early shadows decide what to open and close.
Pastures crack down to snow bone.
This afternoon I watch the sky pillow over,
pink belly swimming through the sun's milky eye.
Sometimes I think I will never love anyone
as much as this quiet
that asks nothing in return.
My mother wants to move to South Carolina—
I never expected her unhappiness
as just now I don't expect sparrows,
far off in a hungry pear tree,
to wind up their throats and remind me
this cold will break.

And then they do.

Redemption at the Russian Tea Room

"Stay me with flagons, comfort me with apples . . . "

—Song of Solomon 2:5

In my husband's city on St. Valentine's,
the *maître d'* swoops to bow and seats just me:
a table in the middle of the room
packed with couples rich with reservations.

Tureens of daisies bloom in great Midwestern gusts
and tablecloths take flight each time a guest,
who's surely not from here, sidesteps the wings
of the revolving door, and what is there to do

but offer up a toast to her, Chicago,
big-boned, blowsy broad who clinks her glass to ours,
no moll of some goodfella named The Chin
but beautiful butcher to the world, *grande dame*

of groaning board and mistress to the clubby coasts,
rising on high heels of steel: railroad line
and crosstie, sleepers suturing the gut
up from the Gulf; out of the hard-packed plains,

where the horizon's heaped up like a thunderhead
that never breaks; out of swamps, the Lake, corseted
by wind, her incarnation rises so that we,
cold supplicants, pour libations at her feet.

The waitress offers warmth with vodka flights
while next to me husband and wife—long married,
such proper courtesy between the two—
pour tea after the Institute of Art.

The man is proud (the fringe of moustache tick-
ling his lip took fifty years to grow steel gray),
and just today he gave his bride the town,
now neatly folded in a square against his heart:

a map, that worn linen of where they've been.
All up and down the avenues along the lake,
the trees stripped down to ribs and stays, and showed
no modesty at light that first x-rayed,

then stained their limbs, as forked, arrayed, and twined
as leaden traceries in glass. How great
a distance sunlight travelled to this day,
on which I hold the Book of Happiness

in hand, thumbing through the pages for a change.
Even the light bulbs on the Symphony
marquee ignited into halo as I passed
beneath the watchful eye of mermaids, mottled

bluish-green, balanced on the bridge's balustrades.
Their breasts were bared, their only armor scales of bronze—
no figureheads hauled from the deep but guides
to us on shore: *Learn how*, they said, *to be*

two things at once, and not two blocks away
the Palmer House hotel, all twenty-five stories,
rose to her full height, squaring shoulders that
each passing hour jeweled with windowpanes of light.

There, eighty years ago my grandmother,
who died one month ago and whose red hair I will
forever wear, once smuggled in the family cat
when westbound Buster wanted none of that.

(For now think of the kindness of the clerk,
a man not one of us will ever know,
who simply turned and looked the other way
from a young girl who wore a kicking coat!)

Still kinder yet tonight, after my compliment
a woman will unlatch her gold locket.
The twinned halves butterfly apart to show
a daughter's photograph, the child who died,

and somehow, shamefully, above the bathroom sinks
it's she who says to me *my dear, do not be sad.*
Although we seem alone, in truth we're not.
The ones who haunt our hearts cannot be lost.

Later, how glad I am to watch the waiter pull
the table from her booth so that grandchildren
all pile in. We're fated to find comfort
despite such days most marked by who's not here—

the many ghosts to whom we call who do not come.
The proprietress, a sweet, dolled-up babushka,
whose sleeves are cuffed in mink, begins to sing
while pouring benedictions of champagne:

My pleasure, love . . . the pleasure is all mine.
She dips to pour, then twirls, bottle in hand.
My pleasure, she repeats until our glasses swim
with stars, their constellations maps to lead us home,

and, oh, for once to know a luck beyond compare.
Lemon medallions shine at each table,
and gilt-edged plates set just for us offer
a sweetness almost unimaginable.

Fincastle Easter

Home for spring and healthier now,
I let my parents fight their own private war
over the leg of lamb, my father unwinding
the thin rope from the roast that sits
like a fist of muscle on the marble island
in my mother's kitchen. All day long
I have been content to walk the dam
between the spring and creek,
where lime grass thickens
to a bed of tulip stalks.
I see now my loneliness was an open hand
into which I placed mine, and
my parents did not do this to me,
and the land did not do this to me.
Only the still-white sycamores
are so much to be up against
while they fill the sky with their lean arms
and refuse to bud or bloom.
Like a wishbone, my heart breaks once.
Before the night is out,
my father carves a little sunset
of lamb slices, and out in the driveway
I peel my best friend's hand off the vinyl car-seat
and say *I'm trying to hold your hand* and
If you want to do this, why aren't your lips moving?
He tries to kiss me, but it feels
like he's trying, and my grandfather,
whose red cane has been hooked over the grate

in the dining room all evening,
and my mother & father walk outside.
My grandmother has been gone for two months,
so my grandfather reaches around me and whispers
I wish she were here to love you.
My whole family looks up into the terrifying sky
at a comet we will never again see
in our lifetime, so we just stand there,
taking it all in: something so bright there
that is so far from us here.

Summering

At the Browns' house in Baltimore,
I was the house-sitter,
jilted and heartsick in the heat and humidity—
Joyce and Eddie long gone
to wear out the summer in Maine.
I'd worn out my life and wanted theirs.

Shock collars kept their dogs
in the rambling yard all day.
There was cable TV, no air conditioning,
five apple trees, one red fox passing through,
and a twisting stairwell in back,
where death whispered, a masked man

on the landing with a knife.
Nightly I climbed the stairs,
wanting his sudden kiss
to save me from the slow month
and the boy I loved gone for good
while I went on, fanned to flame

and heaping up loneliness like laundry.
Instead, another man arrived just in time—
James Earl Jones and his TV crew
shooting the Friday night lineup.
The set designer found a snakeskin under an azalea
and wore it, a shimmering stocking

around her pale neck while she walked
in platform shoes three inches
above the marble floor.
For a year I had slept the dreamless sleep

of the heavily medicated. That night I quit
the sleeping pills, told myself

what warmed me so was the body that loved me.
Downstairs, the dogs stirred and stretched
in their green beds. The floor fan hummed,
the light over the screened door shone:
I could not rest, so I went down to the kitchen
and curled by the bloodhound.

When for some time your life has been a thing
you might not keep, you take it back in fits.
Something newly heavy was in my arms—
a dog who smelled utterly, beautifully of dog.
What do they know,
those who must only have life to want it?

The night boiled on, two sleeping dogs
breathing in the airtight kitchen.
Truck lights broke the dark before day did.
The morning began with the Haitian housekeeper
found murdered at the Belvedere Hotel.
Two detectives cruised the long drive outside

in an unmarked Chevrolet.
Filmed in an overhead crane shot,
they did it eight, nine times to get it right,
then walked from the car, past boxwood
to the front door, which opened
on James Earl Jones looking directly at the camera.

His daughter waited in the catering tent,
sat in the director's chair and ate fresh fruit.
It was his chance to speak. I wanted him
to open his mouth and begin
the slow, difficult dialog of truth.
Something crucial was about to happen:

I stood in shorts, barefoot in the threadbare grass,
and watched it in black and white on the monitor.
I already knew, but not *how*.
The dogs paced their chain-link kennel in the garage.
The location director, whose name was Larry,
answered only to Plato. Because I was half in love

with anyone, I stood to his right and clenched his arm.
The detectives waited, taller in life than they looked
on screen. It was time for James Earl Jones to say
what had been done.
In the script it is fall:
a girl is dead and we must know why.

Ways to Consider the Summer

Only now do I come and go
like a story circling back on itself,
so why shouldn't you think nothing much happened

when I can't explain afternoon's drag into the trees,
stillness's hover like a dog that may or may not bite?
The asphalt breathed heat until its black knuckles shone

and the heart of everything turned to vapor.
It was this way all summer
while I went on breathing in and out.

I learned to float over a core of sadness,
something solid I clung to
like the world between its poles

or a bruised peach to its pit.
You weren't there to see the sneakers
open-tongued in a neighbor's window.

I watched them one evening, expecting their retreat
or leap. You see, they were positioned perfectly:
both of them were perfectly empty.

Late Swim

– For G.C.

The mosquitoes come out at night
and orbit the kids sailing on skateboards
down Kansas Street to Main,
where they light cigarettes and loiter
at picnic tables anchored in concrete.
There they plot escape

under old man Carius's unblinking, blue eye
as he leans, arms crossed, against the rail,
lording over his empire
of hotdogs and root beer floats
like Croesus when the minting business was brisk.
His domain hogs two town blocks

across from the Brass Bull
(where dads who sell insurance & Chevys
shoot darts by night)
and the storefront, now dark, of Ray's Hairport
(the *Playboys* folded into *Field & Stream*).
Wind from the west snaps like a sheet on a line,

rattling cicada shells stuck to window screens,
and the girls taking orders are so bored
first period Algebra looks like a reprieve.
They'll be glad when the stand
is shuttered for the season in a week.
For now, the boys slurp soda pop down to the dregs,

talk about how they'll never live someplace again
where all they hear at night are barking dogs
and the jangle of wind chimes;
where there's no place to go but here
or the basement of Calvary Baptist for youth group,
but they can't drive yet & they don't give a rat's ass

about getting saved, so they shut their eyes
and picture the second coming
of the homecoming queen, who's knocked-up
but doesn't know it yet. She'll be graduated, married,
and divorced within the year.
For now she's thin, bronze as a penny from the tanning bed

as she leans against the juice bar at the new Gold's Gym
and surveys the merchandise:
guys girdled with muscle belts and bulked up
on creatine until their biceps pump
with ambition and buying power.
Later tonight when the town's shut down,

the kids will surf the wide, straight streets
named for states they've never seen,
scale the chain-link fence to the county pool,
a tinfoil glare on prairie afternoons,
and shed their cutoffs as fast as their pasts.
They want only one thing, and they think

they will get it, if not this year then the next—
in two strides now they lope across all fifty states
of America stenciled on asphalt
behind the elementary school.
The country's not going anywhere, but they are,
and their future's idling just beyond the streetlight,

as predictable as the moon waiting to rise,
so they dive again and again
into that chlorinated lake of light,
four feet down in the same old soil,
and they can't be quiet about it
because they are saying goodbye.

What do they care? What do they care
when most nights the cops don't bother
unless a neighbor complains?
And anyway, out here a kid
can see what's coming
long before it gets there.

Dog Days

It wasn't what I thought it was
nights I sat up late, listening to my parents.
Dog days, they said, meaning the month
we had to swim through
like wet retrievers paddling
the reflecting pool of summer afternoons
until we reached September's distant, dry shore.

They were the days dogs carried an odor
as they hauled their hairy, heavy selves
into the damp cave yawning under the porch
or lay panting, laboring, snoring where they were,
flat-out on the sidewalk; they were
days when summer dragged
on, not going gracefully—out of loyalty

or persistence, I do not know.
They were days only dogs
seemed smart enough to sleep it off,
whimpering their doggy dreams.
They were slow days dog claws did not click
as they did not follow me through the house
where I was alone and there wasn't a thing to do,

days I was sent outside to play
until the shadows stretched their long arms
and called me home. It was the season
bees rattled in the windfall crabapples,

insufferable days I was put to bed
while twilight burned, not yet dark—
an injustice when I could hear adults talking

on the screened-in porch.
Their words lived a second life,
drifting through my window,
where dusk draped her loose gown,
a lavender silk scissored by the snap of bat wings.
Dog days, they said, an invocation, a command
for summer to heel, sit, stay, obey,

but already the mild, dreaming world was turning,
writing its own translation of itself,
which in any tongue surely means goodbye.
Sirius was swimming away,
pulled into night's riptide, leaving us
to our own diminished light here on Earth.
In the morning the weather broke,

and when I woke the trees spoke in tongues,
their leaves so glad to be alive again,
and their words and my parents' now made sense.
I knew then, at last, day after dog day—
tongues lolling—would come wagging, bounding
to greet me. I thought *here they come,*
not knowing I was already watching them go.

We Are Easily Reduced

Months after hunting season, my father's dog pulls them
from the scrubbed winter fields. Their bodies
borne back piecemeal—deer hock in front of the garage,
nub of horn in the barn, hoof on the back porch.

Fur scoured clean, they whiten in the underbrush
beyond the bristle of a nearby hill
and in clearings, where pockets of orchard grass
covet a chalked hip. She retrieves those

shot and left to die far past the creek's quick song—
no easy distance for her to drag, bone by bone,
such animals back to us,
and she must climb the ridge where my horse threw me,

opened against the ground, face scraped clean,
perfectly blank, my mouth—a brilliant stain.
At the hospital, I felt the fact of my skeleton charted,
my brain stenciled on graph paper.

Yesterday, my father walked from the doctor's office,
where we waited to hear the news,
took me in his arms,
and gathered me like splinters of his own body.

The Sick Dog

Sweet pagan heart, Diana of the hunt,
we keep you tethered close to us, slow of
foot, mortal, earthbound, golden girl who once,
a copper bolt, plucked a duck from the blue

sailcloth of sky to feel its emerald throat
pulse within your own; at whose approach
tall grasses part, where in summer fields sleek
creatures lived and died according to your

quicker unblinking eye, though the bright blood
on your tongue these days is oftener your own
as you erase the trace of everywhere
you've been and bled throughout the house, such dull

quarry for a dog like you. Shaved and stitched
where sunlight once fastened to your fur,
a sticky burr not even night pulled clean—
your coat of flame the chattering class of birds

embroiders into nests, entwining fur
as if the world were able to rescind
each hard-fought loss and make good use of us,
as if whatever's lost could be retrieved

again. It can't. Listen, if we are saved
at all it will only be by bird beak
and black wing, wren and starling, junk birds that
scavenge the yards at dawn while you watch on

in silence and suffer us our science
as well as our mild God, in whom you can't
believe as you already know how this
will end. Futile the blessing of the priest's

pale hands upon your muzzle when a bone
would be better and more honest at least
for such a wise, all-knowing augurer
of wind and architect of lesser fates

we do not mourn: ruffed grouse or groundhog's neck
in that unholy vise of your gray jaw—
so it comes to all, if not violent then
violated. Rolled over, your stomach's

a map of cancer, cutting, and metastasis.
Where you rest a dark stain seeps. High priestess
of brindled woods, where late you read the runes
of horn and hoof, leaf-litter and twig-snap,

where shadows spill, black hieroglyphics written
by the trees that you alone were born to translate:
love and grief, two sides of the same green leaf.
Here, lace your step through rushes where geese roost,

past oak roots knuckled deep into the banks
of silver lakes returning now to us
as mirrors of their own making. At dusk
the little lights that lick across the lake

come on whether we're here or not. For now
we are. Be glad. Travel until the day
pulls in her sail, sails on. Beautiful girl,
wherever you're going, I'm going there too.

Fin de Siècle

Once and only briefly, on vacation to my parents'
azalea-besotted second act in the low country,
my marriage ended under the whitewashed eaves
of a carriage house while the Saran-wrapped still life
of cocktail hour looked on—a checkerboard
of cheese and crackers, an ice bucket silvered
with tributaries of condensation.
In the bath, a phalanx of tiny toiletries
awaited marching orders, but it was I who left.

Virginians, the new world had grown old,
and the family crest now flew under the banner
of Adams, our English Setter, his tail a streaming flag
and his all-knowing nose, blood rose, the needle
of a compass pointed dead south. He was
Virgil pointing us into fields foreign and flat,
sentinel of the air rent by rifle crack.
Mouth melting on the neck of fowl
and buttered biscuits,
he took his bowl of water on the rocks.

My parents retired to the bar in the big house
to watch the Pocotaligo River turn buttery gold
in the setting sun like a tide of Chardonnay
poured by a benevolent God in the beginning
or middle of our lives, while I waited
on a brick-cobbled patio with the good sense
to crumble—patrician outcropping of oyster shell
at the edge of backfilled rice fields.

I was already on an island of my own making
and later still would be officially banned

as bearer of an unhappiness as water-logged
as night's indigo mantle of humidity and salt
and insect hum we wore and breathed and called the air.
(Ships sailing up the James long unloaded ballast
to rise to reach Richmond.)
Lord, can anyone rescue us from ourselves?

Come dark on the levees, gators climbed
out of centuries adrift in a brackish dusk,
slapped down scaled hides and slept like slabs
with one eye moving—a yellow knifepoint
piercing the horizon. For an hour, two at most,
that night I thought I belonged to no one
and to no place, blind to the way we become
our own memories' afterthoughts:

The scrub pine and leaf-slick of woods,
deer stand I climbed to read away the rain,
hayfield in fall my red dog stitched behind her as she went—
until it seemed I did not remember them,
but they, in the desolation of forgotten places,
brought me into being.

Long after I would be forgiven and would forgive,
myself (after all, only a person much loved
can feel that sorry for herself), the alligators,
primitive prophets of what would come to pass,
would outlast us, too, at our end
when we watch film after film of our lives,
our faithlessness in those who loved us most,
unscroll in a language we no longer understand.

Notes

"Still Life with Jackie O": After the 2001 Metropolitan Museum of Art exhibition: "Jacqueline Kennedy: The White House Years—Selections from the John F. Kennedy Library and Museum."

"Circe and Her Lovers in a Landscape": After the Italian Renaissance painter Dosso Dossi's "Circe and her Lovers in a Landscape," at the National Gallery of Art, Washington, D.C.

"The Apprenticeship of Jelly Roll Morton": After Romare Bearden's collage of the same title, which appeared in the retrospective exhibition, "The Art of Romare Bearden," at the National Gallery of Art from September 14, 2003—January 4, 2004.

"In the beginning all America was Virginia": William Byrd II (March 28, 1674—August 26, 1744) was a planter and author from Charles City County, Virginia, and is considered the founder of Richmond, Virginia. He famously wrote to the Earl of Orrery, "Like one of the patriarchs, I have my flocks and my herds, [. . .]we sit securely under our vines, and our fig trees."

Architectural historians Therese O'Mally and Marc Treib describe Byrd's elevated estimation of the State of Virginia: "Byrd frequently employed both biblical and classical allusions in describing Virginia; it became commonplace to cast the New World as both Eden and Arcadia, the Promised Land and the Hesperides."

"Jefferson's Daughters": I could not have written this poem without the generous assistance of research librarians at the Thomas Jefferson Foundation. My poem's epigraph is taken from Robert Haas's poem "Monticello," which appeared in *Praise* (The Ecco Press, 1979). My poem, including its closing, is a response to Haas's "Monticello."

"The Norfolk and Western": For my dear friend Stuart, who first took me to see the renowned railway photographer's work at the O. Winston Link Museum in Roanoke, Virginia.

No other railroad is more synonymous with Virginia than the Norfolk & Western, which was formed by more than two hundred railroad mergers between 1838 and 1982. Its headquarters were in Roanoke, Virginia, for most of its 150-year existence. The company was famous for manufacturing steam locomotives in-house at the Roanoke Shops. Around 1960, N&W was the last major American railroad to convert from steam to diesel motive power.

"Delay at Washington National": On Monday, January 1, 2007, *The International Herald Tribune* published "A Grim Milestone in Iraq: 3,000 American Deaths" by Lizette Alvarez and Andrew Lehren. Alvarez and Lehren write: "This spike in violence, which has been felt most profoundly by Iraqi civilians, who are dying by the thousands, has stoked feverish debate about the nation's presence in Iraq. [. . .] If the conflict continues into March, the Iraq war will be the third longest in American history, ranked behind the Vietnam War and the American Revolution. President George W. Bush did not specifically acknowledge reaching the milestone of 3,000 American deaths, but a White House spokesman, Scott Stanzel, said the president 'grieves for each one that is lost.'"

Acknowledgments

I am grateful to the editors at the following journals for first publishing these poems:

"Still Life with Jackie O," *The Antioch Review*

"Between us the Sea: Circe's Aubade" and "Honeymoon in the New World," *Nimrod*

"Circe and Her Lovers in a Landscape," *Connecticut Review*

"Lesson," *Connecticut Review* and *Fairy Tale Anthology*, Rainbow Crow Press

"Anniversary" and "We Are Easily Reduced" *Arts & Letters*

"The Apprenticeship of Jelly Roll Morton," *Callaloo*

"Red Nails," *Vox*

"Minnesota Multiple Personality Indicator, et al.," *Redheaded Stepchild*

"Jefferson's Daughters," *Shenandoah*

"The Norfolk and Western," *The Carolina Quarterly*

"Delay at Washington National," *The Chronicle of Higher Education*

"Autumns," *The Hollins Critic*

"West Virginia," *storySouth*

"Resolution in Winter," *Southern Poetry Review*

"Fincastle Easter," *Meridian*

"Summering," *The Chattahoochee Review*

"Late Swin" and "Dog Days," *Connotation Press: An Online Artifact*

"The Sick Dog," *The Hopkins Review*

My great appreciation also extends to *The Comstock Review* & Astounding Beauty Ruffian Press, which wonderfully and graciously published chapbooks of my poems.

I am most grateful for the generosity of those bighearted folks at the University of Wisconsin Institute for Creative Writing. My appreciation goes to the entire faculty, revered guides each and every one, especially Ron Wallace and Jesse Lee Kercheval, who not only made my fellowship year possible but also my hope of becoming a writer. I am also thankful for the friendship of Danielle Evans, Sean Hill, Derek Mong, and April Wilder.

Dear to my heart is the creative writing program at the University of Virginia for showing me the way and then encouraging me to follow it. Beloved poetry teachers Rita Dove, Lisa Russ Spaar, and Charles Wright, and mentors in the fiction program, Sydney Blair, Deborah Eisenberg, and the late Douglas Day and George Garrett remain models of elegance and grace on and off the page. Their enduring work guides me. I count my lifelong friend, the talented Melissa Kirsch, among the many gifts Charlottesville bestowed.

My time at SMU proved invaluable in the completion of this book, and I'm indebted to my first-reader and kindred spirit Jennifer Cranfill. The support of Ezra Greenspan, David Haynes, Nina Schwartz, and C. W. Smith allowed me to balance my loves of teaching and writing. I can't think of a nicer group of people to work for.

A wellspring of gratitude and admiration goes to my dear friends in the Old North State: Richard Vela, Catherine Parisian, and the inestimable McCorkle sisters Of Lumberton, Jan Gane and Jill.

I thank Richard Mathews and Erica Dawson at the University of Tampa Press for the care and thought with which they brought my book to life—and, in a way, me with it.

And finally I extend my love to my family for their abiding belief: my sweetheart Greg Carter; my mother Carol Key, whose support steers a way forward; my late father Tom Key, forever enfolded deep in the heart; my Aunt Carolyn and Uncle Jim; and my in-laws, Mary and Prentiss Carter, who have only ever shown me love and generosity.

About the Author

JENNIFER KEY is the winner of the Tampa Review Prize for Poetry and a former Diane Middlebrook Fellow at the University of Wisconsin's Institute for Creative Writing. She was educated at the University of Virginia where she was a Henry Hoyns Fellow. Her awards include *Shenandoah*'s Graybeal-Gowen Prize for Virginia Writers, the *Southwest Review*'s McGinnis-Ritchie Award for Fiction, and the Poetry Center of Chicago's Juried Reading Prize. Jennifer's poems have appeared in *The Antioch Review*, *The Carolina Quarterly*, and *Callaloo*, among others. She lives in Asheville, North Carolina, with her husband.

About the Book

The Old Domonion is set in Adobe Jenson Pro types, Robert Slimbach's typefaces based on the Venetian roman letter forms of Nicolas Jenson and the italic of Ludovico degli Arrighi. The book was designed and typeset by Richard Mathews at the University of Tampa Press. It has been printed on acid-free, recycled paper in support of the Green Press Initiative.

POETRY FROM THE UNIVERSITY OF TAMPA PRESS

John Blair, *The Occasions of Paradise**

Jenny Browne, *At Once*

Jenny Browne, *The Second Reason*

Christopher Buckley, *Rolling the Bones**

Christopher Buckley, *White Shirt*

Richard Chess, *Chair in the Desert*

Richard Chess, *Tekiah*

Richard Chess, *Third Temple*

Kevin Jeffery Clarke, *The Movie of Us*

Jane Ellen Glasser, *Light Persists**

Benjamin S. Grossberg, *Sweet Core Orchard**

Dennis Hinrichsen, *Rip-tooth**

Kathleen Jesme, *Fire Eater*

Jennifer Key, *The Old Dominion**

Steve Kowit, *The First Noble Truth**

Lance Larsen, *Backyard Alchemy*

Lance Larsen, *Genius Loci*

Lance Larsen, *In All Their Animal Brilliance**

Julia B. Levine, *Ask**

Julia B. Levine, *Ditch-tender*

Sarah Maclay, *Whore**

* Denotes winner of the Tampa Review Prize for Poetry

◊ Denotes winner of the Anita Claire Scharf Award